The Anti-Social Network
(part 2)
The End of Humanity

S.C. Merritt

ISBN: 1532950470
ISBN-13: 978-1532950476

DEDICATION

I dedicate my work to all of my new friends who are helping me each day navigate loneliness and isolation.

CONTENTS

Acknowledgments   i

1   INTRO   1

2   THE ERODING DREAM   4

3   SOME CONCERNS   12

4   ADS SUCK   15

5   SOME HOPE   26

6   SOCIAL NETWORKING MATTERS   30

7   A DYSTOPIC ENDING   36

8   WHAT IS AT STAKE?   45

9   SOCIAL NETWORKS != YOUR NET WORTH   49

10   CONSPIRACIES   69

11   ADVICE FOR THE MASSES   75

ACKNOWLEDGMENTS

A goal of mine was to complete a novel by age 30 and then endure a career shift, from entrepreneur, to author. My goal was achieved but unfortunately, the milestone —to publish—provided no freedom nor even the sense of accomplishment that I once thought might foolishly emerge. Instead, my journey has been ridden with challenges. Unforeseen obstacles that I never would have been able to overcome without the help of others.

So, the process is not over, in fact, publishing shorter, more accessible collections of essays may simply be the beginning. As I launch this fifth book, I'd like to sincerely thank the few friends who have supported me throughout—with encouragement, and also lunches— and I'd like to thank my family.

1 - INTRO

It all started with such good intentions.

The concept of modern Social Networking, popularized by Friendster and MySpace, was brought into the mainstream by Facebook. All three sites began out of curiosity and there is no reason not to believe that the founders were genuinely sincere in their interest to bring people closer together. As extreme wealth potential became evident, it is my understanding that the well-intentioned "original mission" has taken a back seat to growth, profitability, and strategies that prioritize user lock-in while leaving people feeling more alone and isolated than ever before in history.

And so...as often is the case in business. Good intentions quickly went astray.

As it was determined that Social Networking could seemingly only be sustained by an advertising supported business model, the experiences provided serve the purpose of shaping people into commoditized collections of data for targeting and experimentation.

It should not be forgotten, that within the first year, Mark Zuckerberg boasted to the public how he could predict "relationship status" two weeks in advance with 75% accuracy. We all possess strange curiosities to know other people, and predict their behaviors, but so few individuals (or corporations) have the capacity to systematically study other humans. In plain English, the true purpose of Facebook was declared upfront, and the "predictive" and "observational" initiatives have become the basis for long-term sustainable growth. In simpler terms: if users can't be shaped and predicted, their business as an ad-broker won't work. I have long warned people about the likelihood for the platform to exist for the purpose of social engineering and human experimentation, but only recently as various controversial— and widely criticized—acknowledgements of the practice were made public, have people finally believed me.

Would people tolerate unethical methods of unpaid secret experimentation and social engineering if they did not feel LOCKED-IN to the platform? Of course not. That growth has continued, and usage has increased, only supports the general claim that the popular sites are somehow exploiting our psychological desire for friendship, and discomfort with isolation. My concerns are NOT FEARS, they are 100% reality. The train has left the station and gone off the rails. Everyone knows it.

On November 4, 2014, a study was conducted to determine which tech company was most feared in terms of privacy. Specifically, the question was asked: in regards to collection of personal data.

45% said Facebook.

21% said Google.

6.6% said Apple.

The survey, regrettably, did not leave room for people to say: all major companies worry me, but plainly, society is somewhat being held captive—accepting a Faustian bargain—by our desire for digital friendship.

2 - THE ERODING DREAM

In a world where people will always struggle to escape their inevitable path, of being average, how do we maintain the American Dream?

The entirety of society needs to be elevated. Such a result will not occur if the status quo is maintained via software that is mis-aligned with the goals of the individual. It also will not occur if Americans are pitted against one another in a constructed game of zero-sum warfare. There is much global wealth to be created—if the non-investor class wakes up—and while implicit in global wealth creation is an exploitation of the developing world, as is, somebody is going to do it. It might as well be the entire country, and not just the very few. Or, we could redefine the concept of economic partnership with developing nations. Either way, the current path of trusting multi-national neo-feudalistic technology companies, is wrong, wrong, wrong.

Businesses have products and services. Individuals have goals and dreams, pursued via projects and tasks. To the extent that we honestly recognize this reality, we will quickly be able to phase out the "broken dreams," "unrealistic goals," and even "destructive desires," that I assure you, are being exploited by Social Media (and traditional media). Those same failed expressions of

4

humanity, are causing depression, polluting your news feed, and holding you back. None of this is by accident. It promotes economic activity. It promotes spending, and spending is required for ad brokers to prosper. Without widespread re-education, we will forever be enticed to chase short-term desires that enrich the existing business models in the world; can't we do better?

Business 101: Exploit the brain!

Much of the economic activity in the world—not all—is based on the exploitation of the brain's poorly formed short-term desires. My critique of Social Media, is as much a critique of the world, but the software we use each day has evolved to encapsulate our most intimate and life-shaping experiences, and thus, Social Media of greater focus as the "true cause," for even problems which preceded its invention. In a sense, my assertion is similar to an acknowledgment that bars and liquor stores "perpetuate" consumption of alcohol, despite our timeless desire to experience altered states (and long history of self-medication). Along the same lines, despite an innate seeming desire to "get drunk," the "true cause" of alcoholism, is not the desire to drink; it is some deep-rooted emotional flaw (mixed in with some bad genes). Obviously, the participants in the marketplace that profit by selling booze, all have great incentive to sell as much as possible. Little incentive to promote responsible consumption. To bring the analogy full circle, Social

Media sites prosper when people feel alone and disconnected in the real world. It is my belief that such disconnection is actually being fueled by the devolving patterns of communication that Social Media sites promote.

Should Social Media be banned?

The abolishment of anything—like the prohibition of alcohol—creates a huge void that usually gets filled, often with unfavorable outcomes. To confront problems —by showing causality to stem from the prominent perpetuators—presents great opportunity, but also great temptation to act foolishly. Prostitution does not end when you close brothels. Drug use does not subside when you make marijuana, or alcohol illegal. In the case of online interaction, irresponsible communication does not end when you regulate providers of communication tools, but still we must examine our behavior and aspire for a world where people feel less alone.

Lets look at lessons that should have been learned from prohibition.

To the extent that a certain "bar" becomes problematic within a community, some would believe that the issue is best addressed by forcing regulation, or trying to ban all bars; I disagree with that approach. Instead, I believe that new bars should be built, across the street, that are incentivized to teach responsible consumption of alcohol; such a view, recognizes that over-regulation, usually favors the incumbents, rewarding those who acted most irresponsibly when the marketplace was unregulated. In the context of digital communication, it is my belief that a new site that challenges Facebook must emerge (and soon).

We do struggle with the near-term challenge of fighting powerful influencing forces in the world that have no incentive to challenge the status quo; increasingly businesses are economically motivated to absolve certain actors from their potentially destructive role in the world. To the extent that Social Media is shown to be as powerful a force as I believe it is, the government could play a larger role in supporting true competition; or at least in the education of the public (as to why there is LITTLE competition). Recognizing economic mis-alignment between Facebook and their own users, is a good starting point for those who are critical of Social Media and critics have shown interest in creating something better. A few years ago a site called Ello emerged. I supported Ello's mission, but I do worry that their solution is too derivative (and thus incapable of enacting real change).

The problems with Social Media are vast and require a complex understanding of psychology, economics, and the competing future visions for humanity. The fact that problems experienced as a result of Social Media are situationally distributed—meaning people in various life stages, and economic backgrounds, are impacted differently—make it a tough industry to criticize. The claim that the existing sites are mere "platforms" is dishonest, but it also is quite hard to explain to the world why.

A platform, in my opinion, should be neutral. In order for one to partner with Social Media sites—and utilize their restricted APIs—the business interests of the corporate owner must not be impacted. Of course, that restriction is logical, but for humanity, it is dangerous.

Social Media is not just a tool, nor a platform.

To better illustrate our vulnerability to the detrimental influence of Social Media, it is worthwhile to look at a more antiquated concept: debt. Already there is a population of thinkers who understand that "debt" is not just a concept, nor financial product, but rather a "tool" to shape society.

Debt may not have began as such a manipulative device, but it is no secret that financial development, and economic activity, are explicitly driven toward "target" rates of expenditure (or indebtedness). Often economic goals are defined by the promotion of various types of debt; such "economic targets" do not equally serve every citizen, nor social class. Essentially, the global financial marketplace, is hardly a marketplace, and more like a spreadsheet, in which certain variables can be tinkered with, outcomes modeled, and then initiatives enacted.

By that example, Social Engineering already has been taking place, and to the extent that people become "aware," people become disillusioned with their understanding of modern capitalism. Frankly, we do not live in a truly capitalistic society (which is tough to accept), but we can always strive to improve.

Awareness too often promotes apathy, and while it sucks to become disillusioned, we must not flock to support conspiracy theories; rather, there must be an awakening of sorts to curtail the ease by which economic models are used to benefit the very few; similarly, Social Media must undergo similar levels of high scrutiny. The goal? In both cases, to become less predictable.

With increased awareness, the marketplaces within which we are vulnerable to Social Engineering, become less exploitable. The marketplaces become more real. To the extent that people welcome technology that privately guides them in support of their privately maintained personal goals, the models used to predict their behavior become less predictable. This is my CORE argument FOR PRIVACY!

To the extent that people privately declare their goals, and protect their interests, the models become less open to manipulation by oligarchic or fascistic interests. The case for privacy becomes no longer existential, but economic and political.

In a sense, it should be quite obvious, that if your opponent in a chess match knows your prior move history (and can process your past behavior into an actionable strategy), you are at some disadvantage. To the extent that people trust their governments, and central bankers, etc..., then I guess things are ok. With a 12% approval rating for congress, great distrust in corporate America, and widespread belief in conspiracy theories, I think a better vision going forward might be needed to restore faith in humanity (and free market capitalism).

My final point is to encourage a closer inspection of what it means to be free. People need to redefine freedom to exclude the "right" to predictably be observed, manipulated, and then offered up products and services that seem appealing. Technology is only becoming more and more effective at "serving people's desires." As uncomfortable as it is to admit to the weaknesses of the human mind, I'd rather recognize my cognitive limits now, than forever sacrifice my potential to genuinely pursue Life, Liberty and Happiness. I don't believe that a government, especially our government, will protect us from invasively manipulative technology, and thus, we must invest in independently designed technology to look out for the interests of the individual.

It must be demanded by customers, and paid for by the end User, and in the context of viewing citizenship as a global concept, the case against modern Social Media, is a rejection of neo-feudalism.

Regardless of what you are told, the existing technology providers CANNOT play both sides. They cannot both exploit you on behalf of their "customers," who are their advertisers, while serving you. Their loyalty is first and foremost, ad companies, and their users, you, are the product. Neutrality on that issue, is impossible, unless you believe in communism, or fascism, as functional systems. Am I suggesting that certain businesses are promoting communism, or fascism? No, but they are demonstrating their belief that such systems could work, if THEY ran them. Not surprisingly, the same individuals behind these organizations, are highly dismissive of similar systems NOT OPERATED by them, but the de facto reality is that we are being Socially Engineered (and it should stop).

3 - SOME CONCERNS

My top two concerns in the world, remain "total loss of privacy," and "income inequality."

My reasons to be concerned are very clear.

With total loss of privacy, we open ourselves to be manipulated by artificially intelligent agents that are incapable of being audited by humans; or possibly at all. At the very least, as of present, with the companies that are on course to achieve such a "technological milestone" of General AI, we, the users, have absolutely no oversight. In a sense, we will be guided through our day, externally, by a company motivated to make profit, and for what other purposes might they want to guide us toward goals misaligned with our own best interest? It remains unclear, but everyone has political ambitions.

To the extent that profit seeking corporations can somehow claim to be aligned with their users—which I find an impossibility—why would we welcome guidance? The benefit will be clear. By not accepting it, our perceived ability to navigate life, will be inferior to those who do. Competitiveness and a perceived improvement in life, will remain the top two drivers of head in the sand acceptance of Social Engineering.

The total loss of privacy will facilitate advisory services, and to the extent that privacy is lost ONLY to one, or a few, companies, the advisory services will be absent of competition or comparison. Only for those who continue to disbelieve in Artificial Intelligence as a near-term reality—which has to be a dwindling community—should this concern not be near the top of anyone's list.

With income inequality, the obvious concern is that the government is co-opted by the wealthy (through various methods). At the very least, most of the public believes that wealth has undue influence over the political process. Democracy aside, my top concern with income inequality, is that it will continue to widen until it stretches the human species to a breaking point. Such division between the haves and the have nots—with no tools to reign it in—will force us to redefine what it means to be human. Tiers of humanity will not just be observed, but welcomed. As people live different lives, and are held back by different constraints, they suffer in ways unlike their "peer humans" who happen to have a lot more, or a lot less, wealth. In a sense, we will have fewer and fewer shared experiences, and thus the erosion of shared goals, shared ideals, or a shared sense of purpose. Ironically, as a result of our enticement to "share our lives with friends," the concept of a "shared pursuit of happiness and opportunity," becomes not just a challenge, but impossible. I know people believe that we won't let things get "so bad," but mathematically, if the problems aren't structurally addressed, humans will simply grow apart. As history has shown multiculturalism to have been a far more "real" concept, than competing claims to that we are increasingly "melting" into a single cultural identity (at least in the modern world), it almost seems like we welcome the economic divide as a side effect to our indoctrinated desire to "celebrate" who we are, rather than who we could become. By trying to believe that "we" are in a special moment of history, we are overlooking the true reality, that there never has been, nor will their ever be, a shared desire to preserve even the word "we." Those who pretend, will be on the wrong side of history as we witness tragic expansion of class distinction. Those who focus on trying to speculate and minimize specific events, are missing the obvious structurally designed divide which is prepped and ready to grow larger.

4 - ADS SUCK!

Are people really that comfortable with Facebook being the ONLY Social Network?

No. Ello, a new social network that launched with an anti-advertising strategy, was seeing new signups at a rate of 35,000 people per hour.

Will Ello save the day? I am doubtful, but who knows.

So what large obstacle must Ello overcome to gain traction?

Is it our love for the status-quo? Or our laziness? Or must they overcome the ability for Facebook to manipulate users to stay within their walled garden?

Maybe it's none of those things.

Maybe as a result of the public being uneducated about the concerns for a technological overlord, an "ad" supported business model, is of low concern; after all, ads are infrequent, and thus I would speculate that people discount the role they play in their lives.

Already, the evolution of the TV industry, confirms pretty clearly that people will tolerate much, to get something for free. There is SO MUCH wrong with the future visions of the leading technologists, and from my assessment, Ello addresses very little, unfortunately.

They claim that people are the "product," but those claims only resonate to the extent that people understand what that means. In a sense, Facebook serves up user's to be interrupted, and such interruptions are tolerated for no reason; but so many other issues in society are also tolerated. For example: how many people readily accept the idea that politicians are essentially global farmers for the Oligarchs? Not many, but our relationship with unpopular and detested politicians is indicative of widespread head-in-the-sand thinking. Apparently, it has become too easy for governments to point to the benefits and services they provide, just as it is too easy for Facebook and other Social Media sites to highlight the features offered (in exchange for the acceptance of advertising). There must be a greater focus on the non-productive and destructive nature of consolidated power (relevant to Social Networks and government); a highlighting of the coercive tactics used to prevent choice, and the risk of potential abuse.

I will attempt to make a case for Ello's "ad free" mission

Ad supported communication platforms do pose a grave risk in the future. Specifically, as we have already seen, they encourage private tinkering with our emotions and other forms of Social Engineering. As the primary revenue source is advertising, the desire to grow profits, incentivizes the software designers to optimize for maximum exposure to ads; increasing our frequency and duration of use is prioritized over creating a quality experience. Who knows how to define quality when it comes to a brand new service like Social Networking? The optimal Social Networking experience—to maximize pleasure derived from social relationships—might be just 1 minute per day. Or maybe, pleasure should not be how we assess the quality of our experience, but rather, outcomes. As is, with an ad-supported free model, no incentive exists to develop *more efficient* methods of communication. As is, our indoctrinated understanding of happiness, and our observable desire to maximize it, is being arbitraged, by the true desires of the technology creators, which is to create long-term shareholder value (which mostly correlates with long-term, defensible streams of high-margin revenue...or simply put...profits).

I could list dozens of disappointing limitations of an ad-supported Social Network. I will list 8.

1. Incentive to excessively log our behaviors including coercive methods to impose highly invasive terms of service that demand greater amounts of personal information

2. Profiling of users by advertisers (institutionalized stereotyping)
3. Incentive to encourage consumerism
4. Incentive to promote materialism and social competitiveness
5. Sensitivity to the needs of the advertisers (not the users)
6. Incentive to behaviorally drive us into "buckets" defined by how advertisers see the world
7. Incentive to redefine what we consider "virtuous," to support the concept of advertising (idealizing youth, beauty, wealth, and other unrealistic, uncontrollable, and often empty pursuits)
8. Incentive to keep the population dumb, impressionable, and anxious (to increase our responsiveness to ads)

Unless people become tangibly aware of the risks associated with an ad-supported business model within Social Media—and believe that some (or all) of my dystopic predictions will occur in the near-term—ads will be perceived as a mere nuisance; they will remain a part of our world experience as the price we pay for refusing to pay any price at all. If people are too lazy to move their lives to a new platform, then digitally powered ad-networks will be built throughout society to reach you from digital billboards, digital voices, and projected screens placed EVERYWHERE; bombarding us at all moments. The lines between content, and promotion, will continue to become blurred, and it is a question of WHEN, not IF, some influential voice will eventually be delivered straight into your brain.

I am vehemently opposed to advertising, but then again, most people claim to be. How am I different?

I don't know. I really am against it, but do little to fend them off. For a while, I paid for Spotify premium, but when I found out how few people did the same, I returned to the ad-supported version. I told myself that my ad tolerance was for two reasons: 1) to keep tabs on the progression of personalization and 2) to build empathy for those who couldn't afford to opt out. I generally fail to stay in tune with what the masses are experiencing, so consider my acceptance of ads while I listen to Spotify, as a real sacrifice. I know. I'm quite the martyr.

Spotify permits ad removal for just $10/month, but how have users responded? 80% of its users choose not to pay. Does that mean that people love ads? No. It simply means that to most users, removing ads—on Spotify—is not worth paying $10/month. It means nothing more, but I do worry, that our understanding of value, has been skewed. In the presence of cheaper alternatives, like being offered something for free, our brains seem to lose the ability to think. We equate a lower price with "gaining" something, but in reality, the "free version" would not be offered UNLESS we were actually losing something. There is no such thing as a free lunch.

But I like Social Media!

I imagine there are many people who are entirely offended by my critique of their favorite pastime. I know, some people "love Social Media." My concerns are much broader than our relationship with a single company—like Facebook—and I will change the discussion to some older technologies which many can look at more objectively. We have seen misapplications before as other new technologies were popularized; with many of them—unsolicited sales calls, manipulative credit terms, and local cable monopolies—we STILL are working to better align the interest of corporations with those of the consumer. There is no easy solution, awareness is the first challenge, and to gain insight into devious technological applications, let's look at banking.

Money, Banking and Credit Cards are ALL technology

Financial innovations, including currency, debt, and credit cards, at one time were cutting edge technological innovations. Not all innovations serve the population equally.

Debt, properly utilized, can be an empowering instrument for wealth creation. Almost no billionaire created great wealth without the utilization of debt, but typically their use was entirely different than how debt is commonly used by the masses. For example, most billionaires validated their "wealth creation" method BEFORE relying upon debt. In a sense, they validated that their actions were positively creating wealth, AND THEN, took on greater risk—which debt facilitates, to maximize the creation of more wealth. Conversely, most individuals take on debt to expand their purchasing power (a non wealth generating activity).

Social Networking, in my understanding, is a new instrument of debt (including an implicit credit score). Essentially, each user has entered into the following agreement: "I would like storage, and processing power, and software" in exchange for future knowledge about my life. Also, by using Social Media, we are saying, "I would like my reputation to be tradable with others," in exchange for future exploitation that has no bounds. This partnership is unhealthy and dangerous. Debt without regulation, has proven over time to be abused by lenders, as have credit score monopolists, and many other "innovators." That Social Media is heading down this road, to me, is of great concern.

Very little—if anything—has been innovative about Facebook (and their services), except for their ability to coerce people to stay. In a sense, they are a hostile lender, but given the available options, the people still want to expand their line of credit; they want to be accepted by friend and noticed.

But debt is not always bad. Debt can be a good thing!

No better example of how to properly utilize debt exists, than in the case of entrepreneurship. First, most entrepreneurs utilize no debt, either investing their time, or accepting equity investors (which are basically partners, perfectly aligned). As a business grows, debt is safely used to provide "working capital" to make payroll (in advance of contractually bound future payments that have yet to arrive but already are earned); another common use is convertible debt, which again, is a near-alignment between entrepreneur and investor. Only very late in most business success stories, is debt used traditionally (as a loan to make purchases that otherwise could not be afforded). Even with real-estate, developers —and the investor class in general—use debt very differently than home owners. They have business plans that include the use of debt, but they actually use it to mitigate risk while accelerating returns. The focus of debt utilization is not on extending one's financial reach; the threshold of use is determined by cash flow, equity creation, and payback periods. Additionally, corporate use of debt is often detached from the individual, limiting the crippling nature of risky debt utilization from ever personally enslaving them. These distinctions —separating the investor class from the masses—are not accidental benefits. Business schools teach students to properly use debt, elevating their knowledge based beyond *regular customers* who are enticed to rely upon consumer debt for often unhealthy reasons.

How does this relate to Social Media?

Using ad-supported sites is a long-term agreement. That someone MAY shut their account off, is not the determining factor of an agreement being in place. The future of the world will be won by implicit, coercive agreements, reliant upon advanced psychology and privileged information, that are celebrated as brilliant business strategies. It is our jealousy of success and admiration for success stories that prevents people from seeing the cracks in the ceiling of humanity. I am trying to educate people about what Social Media is, by drawing analogies to debt.

Use of debt, without a clear business plan, is dangerous. What is the business plan for most individuals?

There is none. Most people operate with negative, or neutral cash flow, and struggle for their entire lives to build wealth (or get out of debt). For nearly 10 years I have been trying to educate people about the concerns of Social Media, and following is the reason why!

Social Media is the conversion of real-life into a securitized financial product. It is an innovation, like debt. Social Media quantified an existing concept—our real world social networks; in a sense, we all have taken out a loan, with our relationships, thoughts, ideas and time, as collateral. Think that sounds extreme? Already, special apps have been delivered to celebrities and businesses, essentially bribing powerful influencers with more value to keep them complicit to the larger scheme. Similarly, "custom profile names" were first offered to important people, not auctioned, and features are regularly tested by power users, in advance, to ensure popularity upon rollout; but who's feedback do you think is most valuable? Of course, users with the greatest influence, but also advertisers. Notice how no features are priced, or offered based on traditional terms of commerce—like an auction for custom profile names. Features exist to preserve the growth, and control, over the network; resultantly, the long-term objective is to control society.

To the extent that most individuals don't see "the service" in the way that I describe it, does not change the reality. We all have been invited to participate in the use of a new financial instrument, and to the extent that we didn't understand it in advance, nor agree to its future significance, does not change the reality that our widespread participation has legitimized the securitization of every human. Again, the innovation was not the service, but the techniques by which our continuation of the service feels voluntary.

The future costs of such a service are unknown. The present day costs may be measurable!

A recent study has determined that youth today is MORE depressed than during the great depression. I am not surprised. Everyone has been commoditized, and in a sense, reminded that not only will most people never achieve a meaningful net worth, but it has become more clear that their position in life is dictated, and increasingly frozen, by the relationships they were born into; sure, many of their friends, they chose, but such choices were made during their naïve youth; also, nobody told them of the long-term significance of those choices on their future lives. At least not explicitly, with any specificity about the economic repercussions, which are becoming more and more clear each day.

5 - SOME HOPE

How to make a dent in the dominance of Facebook and Twitter? Truly be different.

Ello recently offered a flicker of hope—by presenting an alternative to Facebook—but I have been largely unimpressed. And doubtful that they will succeed at convincing people to change their habits.

Ello promises "no-ads," a transparent business model, and acceptance of fake identities.

I do not believe that their "differentiation" or "new features" are enough to succeed at shifting our attention away from the popular sites. Also, I am doubtful that their "paid feature" business model, will overpower the robustness of the Apple and Google app stores. Or the apps built using the Facebook API. We'll see.

Specifically, advertisements, while annoying, only present an existential crisis. We tolerated them yesterday, so why would today—or tomorrow—be any different?

Additionally, the claim by Ello that "fake identities" is an important "feature," is hard to universally grasp; a few LGBT members were possibly persecuted as Facebook decided to shut down successful profiles using aliases, but in light of the backlash, Facebook has apologized and promised to reverse their policy. In my observation, discriminatory behavior—against small populations online—has not shown to be effective at waking people up to the EXTREME influence that Facebook possesses over the world. Facebook is one of just a couple companies that could become our future digital overlord, and we all should be not just watchful, but actively working to diminish the power of any company that operates with a business model incongruent with the values of its customers. Am I suggesting that advertising is incongruent with the values of everyone? Yes, but that is for every person to decide on their own.

If you buy into Ello's mission, then Facebook and Twitter should probably be avoided NOW...before it is too late. While I encourage us all to spread our personal lives across "as many sites that we can reasonably manage," I am not hopeful that we will. It seems like most of us can reasonably just manage to be active on one or two social networks. Understandably, there is much convenience in using just one site.

Tsu offers a platform where members are compensated for the content they create.

By some estimates, 25% - 90% of Facebook's value is the direct result of our willingness to invite friends and the content we post (as its users). The question then that's worth asking? Do people deserve their "share" of that value? Close to $200 billion by some estimates.

My initial response is to comment on the word "deserve." Fundamentally, people deserve very little. Facebook set its terms—though they do change often—and we supported the site, and continue to do so, so we implicitly agree to their terms. Given the prior public successes at equity creation by eBay (another user driven marketplace), Hotmail (arguably one of the first private social networks), and Skype (a mostly private social network), it at least should have been of no surprise that Facebook would profit hugely off of our willingness to manage our identities within their site. Given that Hotmail was sold for less than $1 billion inflation adjusted dollars (and was a service), and both Skype and eBay had clear business models (which have not changed), I believe the Social Media industry represents an unprecedented exploitation—or capitalization—of psychologically enticed human contributions (perhaps only shadowed by slavery). None of the aforementioned companies—that essentially were valued for their user base, and not profits—were in the business of identity management, and again, it should be noted that their business models were evident and remained unchanged.

So is Facebook's service identity management? Letting us use their site to maintain an online identity that we manage? Or do they manage our identities? And yes, they've added event planning tools, messaging, an API for app development, easy universal login, photo library management, easy SHARING of content and the ability to receive feedback. But for what purpose? Always to further the investment in our projected and accepted identity within not just the digital world (anymore), but real life.

Still, the question remains. Are the users owed anything for their contribution to the value created? Tsu seems to think so. Tsu has created a social network that pays everyone for posting and inviting. Tsu keeps just 10% of the total revenue (from posted content).

6 - SOCIAL NETWORKING MATTERS

Within our lives, there are "rules of engagement." They matter.

Imagine a world were it is the "norm" for your parents to high five everyone they pass on the street; imagine that the younger generation sees such interactions as shallow, or empty, so they begin to improve upon the ritual. How? By ALSO delivering a sincere verbal compliment that is digitally translated and posted on the "high-five-recipient's" public profile. Weird? Of course, but such a community could form. Though I'm not proposing we do so, I can't imagine that such a world with forced politeness would make things worse. Ignoring people we pass on the street, to me, is equally as strange as high fiving them before delivering a superficial compliment.

Naturally, I see the obvious limitations of this imaginary ritual—how exhausting, right? Also, how sincere could one be if they were encouraged by society to be nice? Or how numb would we all get to receiving praise? And so, does that take us back to exactly where we are? Ignoring people?

The main point I'm trying to make is to build agreement that an alternative world—with weird rules—would alter the experience of being human. For those who lived in the imaginary "touchy" new world, or moved there, or vacationed there, their lives would be changed forever. The world in which we live—along with its rules and rituals—defines who we are, how we act, and how we interpret comments from others.

Similarly, the websites we use—particularly search engines, social networks and dating sites—define us. They shape us by their constraints, or by what has become acceptable behavior, and in some VERY CREEPY cases, website operators actively are experimenting with our lives to truly attempt to change who we are. I imagine the known cases of experimentation—by Facebook and OK Cupid—are not the only attempts at behavioral manipulation. In fact, I know that they are not.

If we are effectively manipulated by technology, then what percentage of our actions represent who we are? I'd like to believe strongly in the concept of "authenticity" and "true friendship," but unfortunately, it is my belief that in the wrong environments, those invaluable treasures can be destroyed; or impossible to ever experience; I believe humanity is under attack.

Social Networks are broken and we should care

If one spends enough time in the wrong places, with the wrong people, life can become irreversibly worse. Activities that once were enjoyable—like sharing online —can transform into an experience wrought with anxiety. Personally, I have little interest in sharing online, but also I do not want to become irrelevant. To me, digital life often feels like an endless, pointless, treadmill; or an overcrowded party with drunken, boastful zombies; or lonely, despite knowing that there are people everywhere just dying to "like" or "comment" on anything I choose to post.

Perhaps I am in the minority, but I just described how the "modern" concept of Social Networking makes me feel inside; emptier with each post; more alone with each passing day; regretful that I ever encouraged anyone to embrace this brave new world; wishful that I could go back in time and invest my energy elsewhere.

Why is Social Networking important?

I started in the Social Networking industry as an entrepreneur, and then consultant. I took off 3 years to write essays and novels because I felt like nothing was exciting me anymore. Every consulting project I worked on was related to furthering Facebook's vision, and as you may have picked up on, I disagree with what they have done (and what they appear to be doing). I share in part, to voice my opinion, but also I have lingering optimism in the possibility that I may influence a better direction for the future of the world. Lastly, and this possibility exists, perhaps I have grossly misinterpreted large technology company's poorly communicated visions for the future. Perhaps by writing, I can be known; and confronted; and set straight.

Why must I stay focused on Social Networking?

Haven't the winners emerged?

Initially, I thought I might pursue a new career in the education field, or in consumer finance, or in some industry that directly addresses issues of health, self-esteem and happiness. Continuously I have realized that there is NOTHING MORE IMPORTANT, NO BIGGER influence in our life than our "friends." With strong friendships, we can do almost anything. With destructive friendships, even the trivial challenges in life become insurmountable. Friendships matter, a lot. Possibly more than anything else in the world. People have various goals, and various dreams. Good friendships can be empowering and make life better.

Too often, I log into Facebook, read posts, and then cynically mutter to myself: "With friends like you guys (and girls), who needs enemies." Of course, I say those words MOSTLY as a joke—and there is no single culprit, so it is hard to pinpoint problematic individuals to defriend. More importantly, I talk to people face-to-face (occasionally), and they are still not even close to the same person—in real life—that they project online. Large tech companies would like us to believe that the online self, is becoming real. It is not.

Facebook to me is a daily disappointment about the world

I certainly have not felt uplifted, supported, or welcome online, ever. In my entire life. To me, social networking, as we know it, has only been a destructive obligation. To me, social networking was presented as a gamified celebration of status that is trending toward a promotion vehicle for materialistic consumerism. Even without Virtual Reality as a popularized concept, reality is for sale, and the lines have been blurred between news and propaganda. The blurring of reality will only worsen, and it is possible that society is becoming collectively sociopathic (by accident). Even that problem, as a former Type-A personality, I understand. I empathize with driven people; I know how being driven can go too far; fortunately, I know that excessive Type-A thinking is fully reversible. As an occasional believer in objectivism, I understand selfishness as a mock ideal, and take seriously that people enjoy acting to maximize their experience of life. But to what end? I have closely explored the possibility that Social Networking has had a very substantial impact on Mental Health problems including depression, widespread feelings of loneliness, and possibly Bi-polarity. If the incident rates of cognitive problems continue to grow—and most people personally know someone, or many people, affected—then are we missing something? Are we in a hole and continuing to dig? I believe we are which compels me to assert that we are spending our time using the wrong services.

If I wasn't ultimately an optimist, I wouldn't share.

It will take many pages for my optimism to emerge, but I believe something far better could exist. I believe that we will look back on what we "accepted" as a social network, and laugh. Like how we laugh at Prodigy (as our first experience of the internet), or floppy disks as vehicles of data distribution, or how email attachment limits used to be set at 300k with the claim that "sharing" has never been easier. I believe in a better future, because it is too depressing to accept that the world will devolve into the dystopic visions that I wrote about as a novelist.

If you like things as they are...well...then keep doing what you're doing. If you like your life as it is, then don't change it. Enjoy the pretentious and socially competitive fabricated stories produced by people you once knew as your friends; embrace the increasing personalization of ads as a necessity for technological advancement; laugh or cry at the polarization of politics; consume, or mock the blatantly fake news; click on, or willfully produce link-bait; enjoy, or accept social casino games and the perpetuation of the concept of lottery based luck as a form of advancement; and most of all, enjoy the future devious methods by which you will be socially engineered (or experimented on).

I'm out!

7 - A DYSTOPIC ENDING

Consider Privacy Gone. Ok. Fine.

Big data already has shown the ability to record everything. Much is now being recorded. In the future, everything will be.

Some definitions:

> **Narrow AI:** task oriented intelligent software that does not understand the big picture about someone's life.

> **General AI:** goal oriented intelligent software that understands people's lives better than the individual.

With those definitions out of the way, what's on the horizon:

Narrow Artificially Intelligent agents that perform directed tasks (like "personalizing an ad", or "personalizing a shopping experience")

After that? Expect General AI agents to perform generalized tasks (like "get this person to spend as much money as possible").

The case against Big Data has to do with how data will be used in the future.

Recorded conversations, messages, emails, travel patterns, etc..., will all be capable of being retroactively analyzed, for nearly free, by robust machines that master General AI. People need to seriously recognize how disadvantaged they will be with their mere human brain, faulty memory, and formed behaviors that will foolishly lead them into traps set by automated, personalized commerce platforms designed based on intimate knowledge of THEM. ONLY THEM. The traps set for other people, will be unlike the traps set for you (and me). Nobody will be capable of making sense of the world or inditing a specific action. Every interaction with technology will be personalized through software that is extremely difficult, if not impossible, to audit.

Why can't software be audited?

Auditing software that *might* be causing some adverse side-effect will require a clear understanding of cause and effect when it comes to behavioral responses. You may respond a certain way because of prior hurt, previous trauma, or a bad upbringing. The software thus does not cause your vulnerability, but it will exploit it. It is quite hard to cast blame on someone for exploiting vulnerability; throughout society we readily focus on underlying causes.

How do we avoid demonic General AI agents?

To prevent software from abusively using intimate knowledge about End Users, people need to have leverage over companies that provide services. The only individual leverage people possess is the ability to switch service providers. Data Portability provides the leverage needed to keep the world safe. See the comparison below between Data Portability and Citizenship.

Data Portability is like Citizenship.

If we had truly open geographic borders, and Citizenship Portability, then states (and countries) would evolve to more rapidly serve their citizens. Citizenship Portability should be viewed along a spectrum. The faster, easier and cheaper it is for people to move, the more mobile someone becomes. Citizenship Portability (or use the word mobility if you want) would lead to higher levels of accountability from government. The biggest challenge stopping Citizenship Portability is social welfare programs. They create an oversized demand, and thus borders need to exist. If citizens could readily move around, governments would be tasked with governing more responsibly, including being anticipatory of predictable market flows of citizens drawn in by socialist programs that are unsustainable. Unsustainable welfare programs would not exist. But I digress...

If you follow the example, Data Portability would lead to higher levels of accountability from software service providers.

Citizenship Portability and Data Portability are both essential to create a Better World.

If Citizenship was fluid and open, governments would no longer be able to milk their citizens like farm animals and draft citizens to fight unwarranted wars of aggression. Corporations act along a spectrum of mixed motives. They would ideally like to be acting as irresponsibility as nation-states, squashing their competitors and milking their customers; in a competitive environment they can't; with competition, corporations focus on their customer's needs and provide fair services. Without competition, they act like immature countries; attacking competition and raising prices.

Without Data Portability—like closed borders with strict immigration laws—the people cannot vote with their feet (or bodies). In the context of my concerns about technology companies, users can't truly vote by leaving (they are locked in). That leaves two options:

1. Complaining, and

2. Purchasing shares and voting as a shareholder

Already, complaints about particular services might make one less influential algorithmically by the service provider, but again, good luck proving it, which brings us to the second option. As a final path of resistance, users could attempt to gain economic control of a future digital overlord, but precautions are in place to block that option already: shareholders increasingly can't vote as a result of different classes of stock. So what's needed for a better future?

A Constitution protecting online communication is essential

We are all investing our lives into corporate worlds without constitutions that have implicitly closed borders with strict immigration laws. User agreements such as the "terms of service" are not constitutions, for two reasons:

1. they can be updated without approval by the users, and

2. they have been drafted to protect the service provider.

If you can't export your "user history," then you can't reject the updated terms of service. If companies selectively decide what "data" you can take with you, they have huge incentives to offer *export* only of the data that prevents their competitors from truly competing. In the real-world, the lack of observable customer movement, does not indicate customer satisfaction; it indicates customer lock-in. An analysis of services would show very limited ability to truly export the necessary data to a competitive service. As Artificial Intelligence progresses, this problem worsens. The

inability to easily and fluidly leave popular services—
like email, search and social networking—presents a
most urgent risk to everyone.

The fact that you can technically leave some services,
doesn't discount how the difficultly impedes
responsiveness to the needs and desires of customers.

Will companies act irresponsibly?

Likely not in the short-term, but long-term corporate
interests are mis-aligned with their users. To the extent
that corporate power grows, the mis-alignment will
grow, not shrink. In the short-term, profit margins and
market share are not the only metrics that matters.
Companies are investing heavily to reduce Data
Portability. The growing inability to move between
services, should be of equal importance to traditional
concerns about corporations—like preventing
monopolies. Concern over monopolistic practices is
widely understood; concern about data lock-in is rarely
given any attention. In the context of Data Portability,
even advantages legally obtained through fair-market
competition, should be governed away. Before it is too
late.

What do companies hope occurs?

Corporations are heavily reliant upon user ignorance. By
the time people recognize the true dangers associated
with the inability to export data, it will be too late and
people will have two options:

1. Accept the ever rising cost of their mistake, or

2. attempt to non-hostily take-over corporations using the laws of capitalism.

Suppose people band together and attempt a hostile (or friendly) takeover of their digital overlord. They will be forced to buy over-priced shares in corporations that run their lives, to then change the business practices which will erode the asset they just purchased. If done, by people, or by a government, it basically will be the final transfer of wealth from the masses, to the few, but it likely will not be attempted; rather, the balance sheets of multi-national corporations will continue to grow and grow.

Are these outcomes overstated?

Maybe. It largely depends on how close people believe we are to General AI. Or how controlling and manipulative companies might competitively become with Narrow AI.

What might bring these problems to the forefront?

It is my belief that corporations are de-prioritizing profitability to hold off until they develop advanced Artificial Intelligence. Should shareholders demand that executives more actively extract wealth from their customers, then the concerns I mention may become more widely known. Presently, people are not paying the true cost of using communication tools; large companies are subsidizing communication tools because people are willing to trade away their Privacy and Data Portability. In the long-term, lack of Privacy and Data Portability will be exploited to maximize shareholder value.

So I am predicting a very costly future public takeover of digital overlords?

Yes, provided the public wakes up to the concerns associated with companies that operate true artificial intelligence, it will become relevant for the public to own that technology. In order to do so, a wealth transfer will take place between public pools of money—likely via government—and likely the transfer will occur slowly. Peacefully. But it will occur. In a sense, a runaway technological superiority has mathematically already been set in motion. There are only a few major companies—Google, Facebook, Microsoft, Amazon, Apple—who have the necessary data to truly deliver General AI. One, if not all of them, will develop such technology, and more importantly, implement it to lock in customers forever.

I often cite the hypothetical question: what would Google's first directive be to a super-intelligent all knowing computer brain. My answer: *the computer brain would be tasked to make sure Google does not go away!*

It would take huge blunders, or revolutionary inventions, to change the course of the future. Both are possible, but to place the future safety of the world on "yet to be invented, inventions" or "human error," is silly and unnecessary. Now is the time to peacefully, intelligently, democratically and reasonably, look for solutions to these long-term risks. I don't believe in conspiracies, but I do believe in strategic alliances that give unrelated groups of people substantial lasting advantages over their opponents (aka customers/users). Make no mistake. Customers of large tech companies, are viewed in an adversarial aggregated sense. Management looks at data as if they are competing with users to extract their money and time.

How can the top-threats be identified and analyzed?

Already the top concerns are identified. Just look at how the investment community ranks corporations. The top-threats to humanity are generally viewed as the most valuable companies. To the extent that a company has a premium valuation, is the extent that the company poses the greatest long-term risk to the concept of democracy, competition, and ultimately humanity.

8 - WHAT IS AT STAKE?

What tragedy may occur in our lifetime?

Global domination by a technological and economic super-structure designed to enslave people forever.

What do I mean when I say super-structure?

I invented a term to describe combined alliances between governments, corporations and non-profits that together serve the interests of the very few. These super-structures are evident today if you were to map out equity ownership and participation in non-profits...it is almost depressing to do so.

What entirely disturbs me, is that such a brave-new-world is being delivered under the guise of philanthropy, charity, and development of under-developed populations. Simply put, countries are being invited—through the promise of communication tools—to "join the rest of the world." Communication tools are not fostering democracy, or true friendship, they are stripping people of their humanity. It is by this reason that this book is subtitled: The End of Humanity!

What initiatives am I referring to?

The impetus in writing this book began as I felt compelled to point out the insincere initiatives by quasi-corporate entities to deliver internet to developing nations. Such freebies, come with restrictions. Such offerings, draw people into a "new" definition of the internet. One that is app focused, and possibly the early signs of a neo-feudalistic post democratic world that is being constructed in the name of free-market, borderless capitalism. Critics may argue that freedom builds with small steps and that communication tools are empowering. Similarly, that democracies may form when people have access to the outside world. Even limited access, but is that occurring? Not even in the "best democracy," America, have our technological tools delivered more democracy, so I have to disagree, in advance, that more digital communication tools are critical to the delivery of democracy.

Democracies are formed when people establish constitutions and when people participate in representative governments. Corporate offerings of any variety—including those masked as non-profits—have one simple purpose. To grow the underlying profits of the corporation...by any means necessary. Naturally, in a somewhat educated world (that is partially transparent), the means "tolerated" require some value to be received by the end-user (in my example, the recipients gain free-internet), but I don't agree that communication is a service to be viewed lightly; I encourage more speculation along the lines of "how dangerous" it may be for so few companies to have full access to our private messages, thoughts (expressed as intent shown through search terms and browsing history), community gatherings (measured by GPS data and formally planned events) and ideas (shared via private documents and posts).

Is a non-interventionist strategy—by the US and global corporations—any better?

By non-interventionist, I am referring to the suggestion that the US ignore the needs and market opportunities in developing nations. It is impractical to desire something that won't happen, but lifting people out of isolated poverty, only to place them in the real-world equivalent of the Matrix, is disturbingly not the best option (and surely any objective idealist can recognize that fact). There are certain educational and communal milestones that a society must go through in order to be capable of protecting their own best interests; either individually, or as a state. Not even Americans have gone through such steps—being educated about the risks—before making consumptive decisions that pertain to our relationship with technology. As educational steps are skipped—by choosing services based on what seems fascinating—people *of course* will respond to invitations to use tools and systems that they don't understand. And they will become hooked, as that is what the services are designed to achieve. And people will become enslaved, right in front of our eyes, and in our lifetime. Even the slaves will know it, but they will be powerless; once we pass some unknown technological tipping point, we can't go back. Slaves to the status quo will be incapable of doing anything to change the world.

Technological enslavement may have already occurred in the modern world.

The mere fact that people will readily "debate" this topic, without researching it first, illustrates the effectiveness by which people can be governed passively via corporate products and services. To complain about technological limits to friends, or even to question the present reality within which we live, comes at great personal cost. There are increasingly limited economic opportunities—within the middle class—so to complain about life as we are asked to live it, diminishes the last currency that people care about: *being liked*. It is so important to know that you are liked, a measurement also provided by the same technology companies I warn about, and in attempt to appear content (and likeable), people stop talking about risks in the world which are obviously present. Eventually, even those privy to the concerns—like myself—will also stop sharing their concerns.

Oh well.

9 - SOCIAL NETWORKS != YOUR NET WORTH

There is a growing misconception based on the idea that "Our Social Networks are OUR NET WORTH!"

It is not true. All value created in aggregate within our real-world networks, is being extracted by the tools we are encouraged to use to manage those networks. Naturally, some individuals are creating value—statistical anomalies—but it is not because of their social networks, it is because of their "actual networks." Value is being created not because of Social Networks, but in spite of them.

Those who claim otherwise are demonstrating survivor bias and have developed irrational beliefs as a result of predictably delusional "self-attribution error." Pioneers who benefitted from Social Networking sites are encouraging people to follow their lead, but such advice is dangerously dismissive of reality. For MOST people, Social Networking sites are hugely destructive to their net worth, and the entire Social Media industry is a drag on society (replacing television as the primary time waster).

The claim that Social Networks are our net-worth, is either incorrect, depressing, or doublespeak. Would anyone ever claim that the United States' greatest asset, is our national debt? Some people do. Or how about how we frequently report that one's home, is their largest asset. Only once something is owned, does it become a net asset. Until then, it is part asset, and part liability, and depending on the liquidity, one can net out the two and determine the value. To the extent that a home is partially paid off, the owner develops equity. To the extent that the equity is greater than the cost of selling the home, the home starts to become an asset. Our real-world networks MAY be an asset, but Social Networks are nearly 100% liabilities with no liquidity and no potential to EVER become assets (in the aggregate). Yes, some people monetize their networks, and profit from their participation with Social Media, but the average return—for the average user—is negative. At present, the negative return is relatively small, but Social Networks have become unregistered securities designed to secretly put us into debt forever, and anyone who claims otherwise is misrepresenting reality.

But Social Networks deliver value. Like what? Happiness?

Happiness is arbitrary and has no externally validated value. Would we pay for it? Sure, so to be happy, has some perceived value, but if happiness is delivered by Social Networks, then our perceived value is being extracted back from the user in the form of ACTUAL wealth (gained by the shareholders). A Social Network is not someone's "net-worth," it is potentially a barometer (or tool) for understanding someone's shallowly defined concept of happiness. Your network, curated within Social Networking software, is building the net-worth of the owners of that software.

My Social Network helps me find employment

Creativity and productivity are measurements of one's employability and Social Networks may contribute to one's ability to appear creative or productive, and even facilitate the ease of finding employment. Such efficiencies may deliver perceived value to the employee, but actually the value is not realized by the employee (or the User of Social Networking products). Any efficiencies in finding employment are realized largely by:

1. The employer, and again,

2. the provider of Social Networking software (like LinkedIn and Facebook).

Often the employers must pay for a presence on the Social Networking sites, so over time, the net savings of efficiency, will be the cost of using those services. The efficiency of the market, will result in no net-change in wages for employees. Will statistical anomalies exist? People who benefit disproportionately by exploiting the new efficiencies? Of course, but on average, NO!

Only to the extent that one has become MORE creative, or MORE productive than others in the world, has your

Social Network become an asset. If you need it in order to "keep up" or "to appear normal," then it is a form of debt.

Self-growth—as something attained with or without Social Networking software—is only valuable to the extent that you are growing faster than those around you. If you are growing at the same pace as everyone else—which on average, that's what's happening—then again, Social Networks are becoming greater liabilities (not assets). Also, I would argue that Social Networking software actually has been designed to restrict self-growth.

How does Social Networking restrict self-growth

Never before have we been so capable of monitoring our lives in comparison to those around us. Without getting too far into this topic, the net result is simple: people are trending toward the averages.

I don't use Social Networking software. Is my "net-worth" zero?

As someone who has not messaged anyone online in almost a year, if my Social Network is my net-worth, then I'm in trouble. I would confront the problem if I believed that my future worth in the world depended on my Social Setwork, but I actually believe the opposite. My future value—aka my net-worth—is entirely contingent on me not using Social Media, but I also must convince you to do the same. It is that second task which makes me quite pessimistic, but still I will make my case.

The entire premise—that your Social Network is your net worth—is wrong. "Net worth" is the liquidation value of one's assets, minus all liabilities (usually debt, but it could include alimony payments, or some other agreement to transfer wealth over time). So what is my Social Network, and what is it worth to me?

My Social Network is one part Yearbook (a collection of memories), one part snapshot of my present place in society (a profile and recent history of posts), and one part gatekeeper. It regulates my ability to communicate with the world. Don't like the term "gatekeeper"? Fine. Let's call it the facilitator to communication in an attempt to appear objective. By that definition, one must accept that censorship and the digital policing of your behavior, are both self-serving attributes that improve your ability to send and receive information to others.

Here is a list of censored people or ideas.:

1. Breast feeding movement (women desiring the freedom to share photos of themselves)

2. Rhianna (nude on Instagram)

3. Risque artwork

...and censorship is a near-endless topic, but I still can't find the relevance when it comes to communication. If behavior is logged—which it is—then why the need to censor anything? Ultimately, in a properly functioning world, offensive behavior online would be treated like any other criminal offense, and people would be held accountable for their behavior; that we are even considering tolerating services that censor and police their users is an entirely confused approach.

But there is a gatekeeper...

To the extent that we are reliant upon Social Media, its role as the gatekeeper (oops, I mean, facilitator), will continue to grow, with destructive consequences to the freedom of individuals. As the terms of service are clearly stated, I dwell not on the alarming and destructive techniques that limit our freedom. Censorship is transparently announced—even as it is arbitrarily enforced. Instead, I am presently concerned with Social Media's economic impact on those who participate, specifically, the negative impact on the net-worth of most users. It is a tool optimized to steal wealth from those who use it, and the tool is functioning as designed.

My decision to remain a "user" is an implicit agreement, and technically we are all indebted through our reliance —to the network owners and its advertisers. To the extent that we are not "compelled" to stay, then sure, it is a voluntary arrangement, but come on...where else are we supposed to go? What other site are we supposed to use? It is a voluntary arrangement, not unlike the decision to rent or own. Individually, both options are voluntary, but combined, they are involuntary.

Let's focus on Facebook, which presently is worth more than $200 billion

Investors certainly confirm my assessment—that we are compelled to stay—by valuing the company as if profits will ONLY continue to grow. In a sense, investors believe that much MORE value will be extracted from our lives, than is required to be spent to keep us using the site. I have yet to receive any payments (nor do I expect to), and over $200 billion in value has been created. Some would claim that Facebook's wealth was created "out of thin air," but the reality is that much more value has been destroyed, than created.

Where did the wealth come from?

1. From competing failed Social Networks

2. From competitors (like Google Plus and Microsoft's failed initiatives in Social Networking)

3. From other ad marketplaces

What about the wealth that is created as a result of the new platform? Yes, there are people who have benefitted:

1. Integrators of Facebook enabled apps

2. Integrators of Facebook enabled websites

Where does all of the created wealth actually come from?

1. From advertisers, and

2. potentially from users (though they have not yet been asked to pay)

In the long-term, more wealth could be created than destroyed, but such wealth is unlikely to be not necessarily recognized by the users; in most cases, the opposite is true. Believing that the LARGE MAJORITY of the aggregate wealth created by the Social Networking industry has not been captured by the users, nor will it ever be, the net gains or loss, thus far are somewhat irrelevant. Wealth is created by transference from the End Users. This distinction is important to my larger argument that Social Networks detract from your net-worth (not add to it).

Let's take a narrow look at just Facebook.

Its $200 billion valuation serves as the premise for my claim that being a "user" is akin to taking on a semi-formal debt obligation. I don't know what I will have to do to remain a "user," or what experimentation I will be subjected to, but whatever comes in the future, is believed to be capable of extracting much value from "somewhere." I am telling you plainly, it is from you, me, and the billion other "users."

As a finance related detail, Facebook is currently earning $3.2 billion in annual profits on $12 billion in revenue. To justify a $200 billion valuation, at some point investors are demonstrating a belief that the company will earn $25 billion in annual profits, FOREVER.

Given that there has been roughly $200 in value created per user, is the per-user implicit debt equivalent to $200? No. It is an open-ended agreement, and the value will be increasingly adjusted based on our demonstrated tolerance, or intolerance, of manipulative behavior.

Each day, we are essentially making "voluntary" loan payments by continuing to share and communicate while being observed. Naturally, through strategic blunders or competition from new alternative Social Networks, our implicit debt to Facebook (and other popular Social Networks) could be wiped out, but there is another possibility. Internal development of new features, could raise our indebtedness; strategic efforts could increase the user lock-in; every investment—like the $20 billion acquisition of WhatsApp—at the very least, is "expected" to be paid for by future extractions from the Users. In case it is not clear, future extraction does not mean "revenue generated per user." It is simpler than that. Wealth from the users is expected to be transferred to the shareholders, somehow. Ideally, in unnoticeable ways.

Wealth extractions will occur at the expense of each user's "net-worth," but the impact each day is fairly nominal and difficult to measure (or acknowledge). And yes, one could make the claim that the loss in per-user net-worth is voluntary, a willful exchange of "economic value" in return for the "service delivered," but I reject such a claim. We have been pushed into debt, in an exchange that I would hardly call willful; we are connected to our friends in the real-world, and desperate to maintain those relationships by any means necessary. The motivation for most people to use Social Media is loneliness avoidance, and we have already paid by sacrificing our expectation of privacy, but many more future methods of "creative payment" will emerge.

For example, we were tricked to accept highly targeted advertising—across all aspects of the web—for the rest of our lives. Sure, I could log off, or even de-active my account, but I can't help but recall the active consolidation efforts by Social Media sites to limit my options; to force me to choose between isolation and acceptance of a business model that I never agreed to. I, like millions of other users, started to use Facebook when there were no ads. I, like millions of others users, was a fool.

Does acceptance of advertising really imply a long-term debt agreement?

Advertising does not necessarily need to raise, nor lower,

the price of goods and services. In theory, advertising allows businesses to reach people otherwise unreachable, and thus permits some businesses to become more efficient and actually lower prices. Up to a point, a business' size permits it to produce at scale, become more efficient, and deliver mutually beneficial voluntary trade: products and services. Also, the ability for new services to grow quickly, permits new products (and services) to be delivered faster and priced affordably (with the assumption that higher sales volume in the future will eventually enable profitability).

There are two problems with these theoretical benefits of advertising:

1. Psychological manipulation is taking advantage of our brain's relatively poor ability to make good long-term decisions. One example is how per-user targeting permits price discrimination (so everyone pays close to the maximum price they'd be willing to pay)

2. As a result of monopolistic tactics and market consolidation, advertising need not be priced competitively, which will only worsen in the future (and the expense of higher ad prices will be passed onto the end user).

While there exists multiple advertising options for reaching the same end users, ad channels are consolidated enough to potentially artificially inflate prices of goods and services. Specifically, large corporations prefer to advertise with scale, thus big brands NEED avenues to reach millions, or billions of users at once. As a result, despite the existence of apparent competition, so long as higher ad prices can be absorbed by the purchasing customer, ads need not be competitively priced.

As a result of the above phenomenon, communication platforms have somewhat monopolized advertising, with the result being that prices are higher and they will only continue to rise. Over time, less value is delivered to consumers than otherwise would occur in a world with competing Social Networks. As no users pay to use Facebook, its value is determined by forecasting the implicit transfer of wealth from its "users" to businesses that successfully participate in personalized advertising to drive transactions. In actuality, the "users" are in fact paying to use the service, as the aggregate cost of advertising is included in the products and services we consume. Those companies that buy ads and fail to get a return on their investment, of course are directly adding to the profits of the ad broker—the middleman—but large multi-national corporations are in it for the long haul, and continue to invest in the value of their "brands." In addition to paying for the cost of driving transactions, we the "user," are investing in the creation of "brands."

So do "brands" lower prices or provide any value to the world? Possibly they allow companies to make larger long-term investments which result in products and services that otherwise would not exist. In terms of another form of "value," trusted brands can save consumers time—and time is valuable—but look to how investors value brands; most companies consider a "strong brand" to be contributory to their long-term ability to generate profits.

With all factors considered, the net cost to consumers being reached within a competitive ad marketplaces should be zero, but as there are limited options for reaching "potential consumers" at large scale, ads are hardly competitively priced. "Brands" have been aggressively competing to reach the consolidated "users" and brand advertising—meaning no specific product or service is being offered—is a $550 billion a year market. That figure is an investment in future value that is expected to be recouped by you and me. The "users." For those concerned, massive amounts of money are being spent, for the purpose of building companies that potentially are diminishing the functionality of democracy and capitalism.

To the extent that "brand equity" is created—by companies that invest in brand building—should not be something that consumers blindly accept as beneficial. "Brand equity" is an observation that consumers will irrationally favor "overpriced" services from trusted brands, much longer than if the brands were never established. If consumers were rational (with access to reliable information that could quickly be accessed before a purchase), then brands would have little to no intrinsic value. Shareholders now value "brands" as if they were tangible assets, but "brands" can only have value—above and beyond the value of the products and services sold—if they serve to limit the competitiveness and transparency of a marketplace. We call our economy a "free market," but it is hardly efficient nor free of massive barriers to entry. At the very least, the world is increasingly being shaped NOT to maximize the "net-worth" of consumers, and Social Networks have played a large role in the progression of this trend. By that reality, my Social Network is not contributory to my "net-worth," and neither is yours.

How powerful are brands? Consider this example. If another free search engine emerged that was equal to Google, and paid us 10 cents for every search we made, we likely would still use Google out of habit and trust in its reliability. That potentially irrational decision confirms that brands do intrinsically matter, but Google is a tough example because much of their reputation was established during a period where little advertising took place; now of course, Google is one of the largest digital advertisers in the world. So, look more closely then at OTHER BRANDS, and ask yourself, does it appear as if people support some "brands" long after the products and services are unique and better than alternatives? In my opinion, it is quite obvious that people have a strange obsession with "brands" that I have never understood. In my opinion, that investors value "brands" to have intrinsic worth, is a direct evaluation of the irrationality of "users" of Social Networks, and consumers in general, that are capable of being manipulated to act contrary to the benefit of their "net-worth."

While I know maximizing one's "net-worth" is only one of many objectives that motivate people in life, no foundational product or service should exist with the potential to systematically extract so easily, gains in one's "net-worth." The whole concept of Social Media relies upon the notion that people will endlessly climb over one another to maintain their position in society...spending a greater portion of their disposable income to do so...than they previously were doing (which already was a lot).

If people truly care about their "net worth," the ONLY hope is to push back against the current "Walled garden" approach to Social Media. Social Media is designed to exploit "users," lock everyone in (possibly for eternity), and raise the price of products and services by reducing the competitiveness of the global ad market. Additionally, Social Media incentivizes materialistic social competitiveness, when in reality, a better system could be designed to leverage our naturally competitive nature while supporting our long-term economic goals.

While any new company could attempt to challenge Facebook or Google, the main point being made is that communication need not be subsidized by ads. Similarly, all complex digital marketplaces should be rejected in favor of reasonably designed services that are transparently delivered through traditional transactions. Now is the time to double down on self-awareness as we charge into the future which otherwise may only continue to become more bizarre and potentially scary. I expect a continued uptick in anti-technological community formation—where people live off the grid to focus on sustainability, or whatever—but for the rest of us who have yet to give up on society, we must work to design a future that protects that which we value. How about starting with ourselves? How about recognizing the destructive impact of advertising on the average "net-worth" of every "user" of Social Media? How about realizing that privacy and freedom from interruption, are both valid and attainable expectations.

Being predictable is a problem!

The collective earning power of the users of Social Media has theoretically inched up at pace with inflation. Not measurably faster, nor slower. If our Social Networks are our "net worth," then future earning potential would be predicted to increase as a result of our participation. More accurately, Social Networks permit OTHERS to predict our future earning potential with greater accuracy. Being able to do so, does not indicate that Social Networks add any value, and in fact, they help achieve "price discrimination," which as I mentioned earlier, is destructive to the "net-worth" of each "user," at least in the short-term. Should Social Networks become relevant in credit applications, or other aspects of our life, it is likely that for some people, their credit worthiness may actually substantially decrease as a result of their predicted inability to properly navigate a world with increased "price discrimination." In addition, the ability to measure "who your friends are," may also decrease your "net-worth," as a structural stereotyping that occurs to punish people based on the "poor company that they keep." There is no solution, other than banning such practices, and I am very pessimistic about any governmental attempt to regulate Social Media.

In many industries, the predicted lifetime earning potential has actually decreased, a lot, as a result of technological innovations that loosely could be defined as Social Media. The formation of digital Social Networks has accelerated the pace at which companies are investing in AI, which ultimately will take us to the technological singularity faster and replace many well paying jobs. As Social Networking has accelerated technological innovation, the likelihood of human obsolescence now seems greater. How does that reality effect everyone's net worth? Or future net worth? The answer is simple: it has a negative effect.

Social Networking does function in part as a Walled Garden platform; numerous services were incapable of being developed until the technology became mature. Value has been created, potentially a trillion dollars, but also much value has been destroyed.

One booming industry is narrow AI, and while that technology (in my opinion) will not diminish long-term earning power of humans, it doesn't matter. General Artificial Intelligence—the singularity—will wipe out all gains (except for those who control it, or control data required for it to function). Whether the technological singularity occurs in 5 years, or 20, matters little. Once it occurs, humans will become nearly obsolete, and yes we will still have our social networks, but no, they will not be worth anything.

Our diminished relevance as humans will occur more rapidly as a result of Social Media's proposition, so let me detail what it has achieved. It has acted as a digital cheerleader, encouraging us to trade knowledge for fame. To share (for free), in exchange for likes. The deal accepted by more than a billion users, will be looked back upon as more tragic than the alleged purchase of Manhattan in exchange for $8 worth of beads and trinkets.

What we have publicly (and privately) shared, will ultimately go into feeding the acceleration of General Artificial Intelligence, so lets look at how we have exposed ourselves. We have conversed, to the tune of over a billion messages a day, and we have created millions (if not billions) of well-intentioned tutorials posted on YouTube and other websites. All data is comprehensible TODAY by machines, and ultimately, the period between 1994 and 2014, may become the greatest invisible transfer of wealth in the history of the world. Other Q & A sites, and wikipedia, all fall into this same category, and yes, they have served us all, but also they have trained our future digital overlord...and now we wait for it to emerge.

A book worth reading is Vonnegut's Player Piano. The dystopic author depicts an automated society that occurred through the conscious digitization of knowledge for the purpose of transferring power from man to machine. For the 1%, society improved, but for everyone else, poverty. Though we currently watch videos (and read articles), ALL of the collective knowledge of the world will soon be codified into software, and in the short-term we will pay (or exchange our privacy) to be guided by technology far smarter than ourselves. In the long-term, we will be governed by the same technology.

The collective knowledge created over thousands of years, has been pushed by billions of users onto public websites and already has been sucked up by Google and dozens of other corporations. Such knowledge—and the labor required to publish it—will serve as the foundation for machines far more capable than us in terms of speed (of course), but also reason, analysis, comprehension, communication and even innovation. Sure, some experts have been compensated along the way, along with some amateurs, but once machine learning is perfected—and it is now close—then what? For decades we have known that computers are capable of much more than just computation and regurgitation, but perhaps we never knew what to do? Without serious course correction, we will look back at our lives and realize: "Wow. We were seriously duped."

The current Social Media sites should be rejected entirely in favor of new systems designed to defend our relevance while contributing to our privacy, mental health, and earning potential (which determines our net-worth). As is, our Social Networks are NOT our "net worth," and as I've already made clear, they resemble an unsigned debt obligation. The arrangement needs to be confronted, and other search, media and communication tools should similarly be reconsidered in favor of new services with objectives better aligned with humanity. New services without user lock-in, should be favored to reduce the exploitative potential of these de facto unsigned debt obligations maintained by psychological and social manipulation.

While it sounds alarmist, society at large should be re-engineered in advance of the singularity, and the event—when computers become smarter than us—should be recognized NOW as more world changing than nuclear and biological weaponry.

10 - CONSPIRACIES

Garbage in, garbage out, and the rise of conspiracy theories

As a result of so many blatant attempts—by governments and corporations—to deliver propaganda, the world has become a breeding ground for the acceptance of conspiracy theories and alternative methods to explain the world. If one is constantly told that individual actions can change one's position in life (and shown rare examples), it builds self-hatred within those who see no light at the end of their own tunnel; paired with that, is often hatred for the ruling class; in a state of constant hatred, one is inclined to start distrusting everything that they once were told in favor of conspiratorial thinking. In a state of distrust with the past, one is encouraged to believe in a promise of a better future (even a dishonest one). In a sense, people are readily open to new ideas, including bad ones, and creative technologists are exploiting the lack of readiness for the "future" with imaginative narratives. Theories, and mythologies, that are equally destructive as the old ones—and untested—are being rolled out constantly; intelligently—or manipulatively—they are delivered in such a way to demonstrate insincere understanding of people's subjectively experienced reality; personalized news, and online experiences, permit the emergence of dangerous ideas; ideas which are being devoured.

What is the most widely misunderstood aspect of our world?

That there are secrets.

There are no secrets. Everything people need to know, is out in the open.

To be encouraged to look for secrets, is a distraction.

In plain English, we are "conspiratorially" manipulated toward choosing actions that make one's life worse, specifically, as already discussed, that discourage the creation of personal wealth. If people were asked, "would you want to live in such a world where conspiratorial forces exist," everybody would answer NO. Well. We don't live in a world run by conspiracies but the known collaborations are equally disturbing. No new secrets need to emerge to make sense of everything, but the answers lie in the dissection—and recognition— that people are deluded and the world is complex.

Potentially, the world is too complex to comprehend. Potentially, the world is collectively insane.

Interested in entertaining central banking conspiracies? Consider that all central bankers and politicians openly discuss just two methods of economic stimulation.

One: Cutting taxes for the wealthy, so the "job creators" can put people back to work.

Two: Incentivizing consumption.

Never is decreased consumption seen as a healthy nor desirable outcome in terms of public policy. Never is there a collective agenda for people to save more. Such a proposed policy is seen as an unacceptable behavior to promote within society; which shows a blatant, out in-the-open, fundamental mis-alignment between society and the individual's long-term economic goals. Not once have I heard people demand from their politicians that such a mis-alignment be corrected. Not once. Maybe that is all that has to change?

Could it really be so simple? Yes. People need to demand that politicians help them spend less.

Always, decreased consumption by the non-investor class is seen as a "problem" to be combatted. This relationship with our government (encouraged by the businesses within it and very powerful individuals who set economic policy) is at best, in conflict with its citizens (by accident). At worst, it is a cruel form of tolerated psychological torture. Still, it is not a conspiracy nor a secret. It is openly proposed, and any opposition is met EVERYTIME with the same answer: "jobs, jobs, jobs." Without consumption, ALL OF YOUR JOBS WILL GO AWAY! It is untrue.

The people just need to say NO, and insist that politicians help them save money. It can be done, and increased personal saving does not destroy jobs. It produces wealth and permits investment. It enables non-investors, to enter the investor class. To the extent that job creation dips, or lags, or does whatever....who cares. Wealth is more important. Joining the investor class, as early as possible, is the American Dream. In fact, it is everyone's dream.

Imagine if Saving and Spending were religious terms (instead of economic terms).

Imagine if Saving was akin to expressing "faith in God," and Spending, a sign that one is "supporting the devil." Now, imagine if politicians openly tinkered with religiosity with the same openness that they talk about economic engineering; I'm imagining politicians that talk about the need to address people's "rising faith," calling faith a bad thing. Perhaps they would justify "faith destruction policies" in order to limit the number of people who would one day experience Salvation? Such an absurdity would be confronted as an evil scheme, but that's because the public understands a simple concept. Faith in God, is good. Devil worship, bad.

Well, economics is not that complex either. Saving money, produces wealth. Spending more than you earn, puts one in debt. Among the investor class, Saving (or intelligently investing) is classified as divine behavior, but this is not behavior that is applauded by the masses. Among the elite, people laugh often at the policy suggestions that are used to drive consumption by the masses; while profiting as well (of course). To those educated, Saving and Investment, ARE divine activities. Only those two methods are acceptable uses for their money. It is the rest of us who are supposed to spend, spend, spend. As is, Saving is almost perpetually presented as an unpatriotic action, and in some cases, we have explicitly been told that Spending is "our duty." I recall being told that if we stopped spending, the terrorists will have won. Not surprisingly, the wealthy disregard such foolish advice and spend only when they believe their actions will result in a return on their investment. Why then is such broken advice—to spend, spend, spend—acceptable for disbursal to the masses? I don't know. Well. I have ideas, and depending on the day, they fall under three categories:

1. conspiratorial,
2. a necessary evil (with no better alternative)
3. a potential flawed remnant of a democratic system that is in desperate need of improvement

As I have chosen to not entertain conspiracy theories, I settle on the conclusion that our outdated policies—which always encourage spending—are a remnant of society that we readily should upgrade.

11 - ADVICE FOR THE MASSES

The masses need to understand just one thing. Save money! Demand help to do so. Hold politicians accountable if they fail to provide help. Results can EASILY be measured.

At the very least, individuals should be invited to educate themselves and understand the behavioral incentives and propaganda—designed by their own government—that influence their daily decisions; policies are openly announced and thus NOT within the realm of conspiracy theory. As is, most policies by politicians are created to serve the investor class; mostly we are encouraged to spend (and not save).

Aside from saving money, what else do people need to prioritize?

People should be invited to explore the techniques prevalent throughout society that undermine their ability to make sense of economics; and perhaps decision making (both in the long-term, and short-term). Knowledge may be hidden, but it is not censored to the extent that it could be. Very clearly, we live now in a society with effective self censorship—as a result of ignorance, and maybe that always was the case—but at least we do live in a country where those with great self-control, can source out new ideas, and try to better themselves. Sadly, however, the deck is stacked against the individual (hopefully by accident). Certainly, Social Media, at best, is an accidental tool to compound the problems, and at worst, a manipulative industry designed to perpetuate ignorance (and fuel invisible class warfare).

Capitalism = Class Warfare. Social Media built the castle walls for the new kings and queens.

Some would argue that "invisible class warfare" is what makes capitalism great. I would have a hard time disagreeing, but I would encourage the teams which are consistently losing the war, to explore new Social Media platforms. Just as we are "what we eat," we also become the product of the ideas we ingest. Social Media is designed, specifically, to feed the world unhealthy nonsense, and again, perhaps it emerged to serve that role by accident. Big deal, so those suffering, are suffering as a result of mistakes. Does that make them feel better? By now—since the Social Media industry is mature—to dismiss side-effects as accidental, is no longer a valid excuse (in my opinion). I expect our technology to be better, and if given the opportunity, I will design and build software to demonstrate ideas that I have worked on. My goal is to first identify problems, address the problems which I outline, and then hopefully help create a better world. As is, Social Media products, in my opinion, are making the world worse.

Power matters. Voluntary exchange seizes to occur

once the power divide grows too great.

The list of potentially manipulative knowledge disparities between Social Media sites and their End Users continues to grow; the mis-alignment of goals between the provider of the service, and the individual, have been not just unaddressed, but actually disregarded through newly formed mythologies. The service—and entire industry of Social Media—has become a celebrated example of American ingenuity; the founder —Mark Zuckerberg—an American success story; the early investors, visionaries. I don't disagree with the validity in recognizing success, but caution the public to not let it become blinding.

How many times must we witness the same situation, BEFORE we finally learn, that some successes— especially the greatest ones—often require subjugation; at the very least, with all great wealth creation, there are painful and lasting externalities that only become more costly to the taxpayer. If you disagree, I welcome suggestions to the contrary, but I am specifically referring to Social Media's role in perpetuating ignorance, fueling hatred, contributing to Mental Health Issues and obfuscating reality.

Permitting people to use "new technologies," even to their own demise, is not a question of freedom or censorship; I am not suggesting that we restrict people's freedom to avoid exploitation; also, I am not confident that the problems would be effectively solved by regulation, and likely they would be made worse; the issue has become one of education. People need to understand Social Media and what it is all about.

Simply put, Social Media is the quantification of humanity combined with the monetization of a centrally managed reputation system (that nobody agreed to). In theory, I object to none of these innovation but I deeply oppose the "behind-the-scenes" development of marketplaces that otherwise would take longer to establish (if they required willful participation). Specifically, I refer to the secret gathering and exchange of data that is currently taking place to help "service providers" better "know" their users. Specifically, it is a problem when the End Users believe the service is different than what it actually is.

Again, I relate Social Media, to debt.

Before people can understand Social Media (which has been mythologized), they must understand the concept of debt.

Traditional debt is a simple example of technology used for both good and bad. Payday loans have recently received long overdo attention for being exploitative and corrupt bastardizations of the concept of debt. As have strange mortgage terms. As have abusive and exploitative credit card terms. As have the use of foreign debt, as an instrument for economic dependence of developing nations. As have micro-loans, as a favorable method in comparison to straight charity. Like debt, Social Media could be a source of good, or evil.

I am not proposing that we ban Social Media (or even regulate it).

The solution is to educate the public. As we now recognize the psychologically manipulative practices used to advertise undesirable products to children—like cigarettes, alcohol, fast-food, sugary drinks and a wide range of other vices—there obviously is much precedent for regulating industries. I would like to believe that I am opposed to regulation, but it does sadden me that we have rarely (potentially never) combatted unhealthy products without government intervention. It would seem like a thinking people could figure things out on their own, but in a country where the state sets the national education agenda, one must wonder why economics, health, psychology, sales, marketing and other highly relevant industries, are absent from the public educational experience.

False mythologies are born in public education

Instead of teaching people how to best navigate the world to create wealth, we utilize our "public" institutions to re-iterate mythologies like "work hard, get a job, buy a home (using debt), and you'll be happy." Such banal forms of outdated propaganda do not take into account the reality that happiness is subjective; happiness is based on what one defines as necessary, and is capable of being manipulated by all of the "skills" that are taught within higher institutions. Further, there is much to be said about "hard work" only being very narrowly contributory—though highly correlated—with one's success. It is all too predictable, to know that one can only "work hard" for so long, without economic reward, before one becomes entirely disillusioned with the apparent mythology that "hard work" was supposed to be the path to success. When so many households are filled with parents who "work hard," but are both poor and unhappy, how do we preserve a "virtue" like "work ethic"? In so many homes, children observe "hard work" to be the cause of unhappiness, and we fail to ever properly explain the confusing nature of the world. In the mind of so many Americans, hard work is no longer believed to yield results. The long-term devastating nature of such disillusionment, is potentially the greatest threat.

So "hard work" does not produce success, should we not work hard?

Of course, the answer is not to devalue the concept of "hard work." It is a virtue and truly essential to one's success, but it is merely one of dozens of factors. To deprive youth of a realistic presentation of reality, and not guide them with accurate theories, or realistic advice, is to undermine their future ability to trust authority (and potential mentors) while breeding laziness. These predictable outcomes eventually result in delusional thinking, if one aspires still to be happy. Is this the goal for America?

As is, we do have a population of somewhat lazy, and delusional, people. You the reader, are likely trying to be the outlier (as reading is an investment in your future), but given the circumstances—and taking cognitive sciences into account—I would argue that even lazy people (who don't read) are likely working as hard as they know how to; or as hard as they were conditioned to work. Along those lines, scientific studies lead me to believe that delusional ideologies make perfect sense given one's life experiences. In a sense, hard work requires a belief in the payout. Laziness is not a trait, but rather an expression of experience. Delusions are not a choice, but an unconscious coping mechanism.

If Social Media, like debt, is a tool that can be properly used (as well as mis-used), then we need to focus on informing people about how to recognize misuse; and garner support from people interested in new superior technological solutions.

We need to educate people on the importance of choosing technology that guides them toward their goals, objectives and possibly even their desires. We need to educate people on the value of distinguishing between needs and wants; on recognizing unhealthy, or unrealistic desires; on setting better goals. In the absence of people willing to recognize their cognitive limits—in comparison to both technology and a class of people who have received far better education—I do not know where to start aside from trying to "identify some of the problems."

We are at a political crossroad where people oddly are willing to fight to preserve the ability to get themselves into debt; and use products and services that make their lives worse. People are taught to believe that accessibility to ALL products and services, is part of what it means to experience freedom; oh how we love freedom. At the very least, people are unwilling to mobilize to confront manipulative lending practices, or demand solutions to their observably unending economic treadmill on which they desperately run (or walk, or crawl); amongst these "free" citizens, the paycheck-to-paycheck lifestyle is validated by their peers; amongst these "free" citizens, the notion of complaining is deemed un-American; so long as people aren't alone, they feel less victimized; similarly, depression is becoming the new norm (or maybe it always has been prevalent, but under-diagnosed). Depression and indebtedness, are both surging.

While mental health is increasingly being highlighted, the question remains, are we taking it seriously? We seemingly recognize Mental Health Issues as reasonable side-effects within a free society. How might one suggest that we re-evaluate the concept of freedom? It is my belief that certain technological systems are potentially depression inducing, but they are incapable of being regulated as they move too quickly. At the very least, many technological systems are mis-aligned with the goals of their Users. How do we move forward in a world where the thinking individual is targeted, and isolated, until they give up? How do we move forward when the broken-spirited "former thinkers" are dragged back toward a mob of delusional, depressed, non-thinking and technologically dependent economic slaves?

What if these mechanized forms of "isolation" and "coercion" are being done by one's own broken Social Network? **Then it is their "friends" doing it, right? And not the system?**

I honestly don't know.

How might a nation become educated about technology and business?

Should I try to reach people, one at a time? Or one community at a time. Or, possibly, to reduce depression, we should report the death of the American Dream by openly identifying our observably tiered social status permanence—which I see as an invisible caste system—to be a reality of the human condition? Part of the American Dream.

We should label class stagnation, and inequality of opportunity, as the result of democracy. Define our present world as "the best we can ever do."

At least by acknowledging reality, people may become happier. Right?

Though I lack tangible solutions—at present—I strongly believe we can utilize technology to create a better world. I believe technology can be developed to truly prioritize humanity, or empower us to go in any direction that we want. As is, the best claim we can make about Social Media, is that it has "changed us forever." Nobody is confident that it has made us better, or will make us better...or let me correct myself. Nobody that is not profiting from its exploitation of humanity, believes it is guiding us definitively to some better future. At best, it has pros and cons, and personally, I believe the balance is largely unfavorable to those already struggling; to the non-investor class. To those encouraged to spend, spend, spend.

I believe it is a right, not a privilege, to be guarded from government propaganda; and warned about technological systems with mis-aligned objectives; and properly educated; and told about even unpopular, or uncomfortable realities. I believe that systems that operate transparently, will promote honesty, and thrive, and lastly, perhaps naively, I still believe that the truth will set people free.

ABOUT THE AUTHOR

Scott Merritt, a former technology entrepreneur, sold a social networking company that was similar to Facebook (it was present at 50 universities). He then worked as a management consultant in the tech industry, and through first-hand interactions with dozens of CEOs, gained insight into the mind-set of the 1%. Observing a disturbing hunger by upper management to automate their companies and obsolete their workforce, he grew disillusioned with the celebrated trajectory of technology. Not only for its displacing nature, but also how it is designed to be not augmentative, but rather, an addictive crutch. In 2008, he foresaw technology's role in the undermining of civil liberties, privacy, democracy, and free-thought, and grew disgusted by the willingness for consumers to accept Orwellian terms-of-service in exchange for the vague promise of convenience...and perceived friendship. In 2010, he ran far from the tech industry...and then began to write. This collection of essays is his fifth publication.

www.ingramcontent.com/pod-product-compliance
Lightning Source LLC
Chambersburg PA
CBHW061101050326
40690CB00034B/1761